★ EASY PIANO ★

33 COUNTRY HITS

WITH

JUST 3 CHORDS

CONTENTS

ISBN 0-7935-8838-3

M1630.18
.A1265
1997x

HAL•LEONARD®
CORPORATION

7777 W. BLUEMOUND RD. P.O. BOX 13819 MILWAUKEE, WI 53213

Visit Hal Leonard Online at
www.halleonard.com

ACHY BREAKY HEART
(Don't Tell My Heart)

Words and Music by
DON VON TRESS

You can tell the world you nev-er was my girl._____
You can tell your ma I moved to Ark-an-sas. _____

You can burn my clothes when I'm gone. Or you can tell your friends_ just
You can tell your dog to bite my leg. Or tell your broth-er Cliff_ whose

Don't tell my heart, my ach-y break-y heart,_ I just don't think he'd un-der-

stand. And if you tell my heart, my ach-y break-y heart,_ he

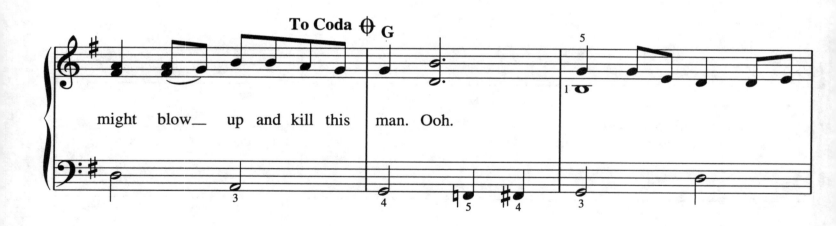

might blow_ up and kill this man. Ooh.

D.S. al Coda

CODA

man.

Don't tell my heart, my ach-y break-y heart, _ I just don't think he'd un-der - stand. And

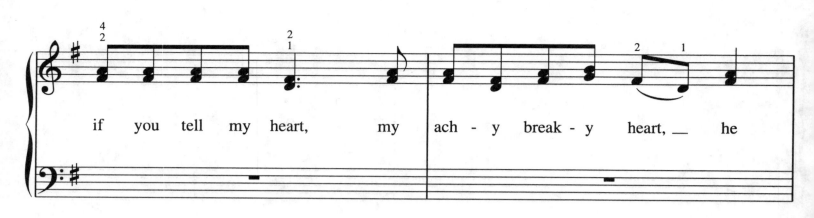

if you tell my heart, my ach - y break - y heart, __ he

might blow__ up and kill this man. Ooh.

7

ALL SHOOK UP

Words and Music by OTIS BLACKWELL
and ELVIS PRESLEY

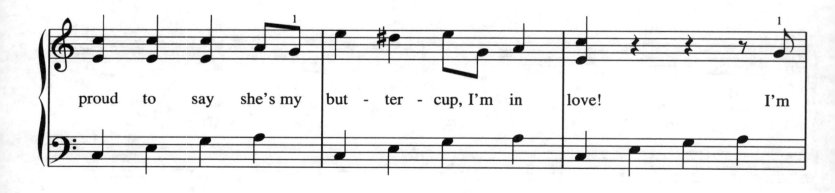

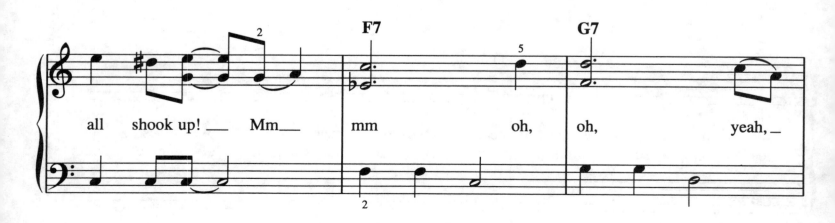

THE BATTLE HYMN OF LOVE

Words and Music by DON SCHLITZ
and PAUL OVERSTREET

Bright Country 2-beat

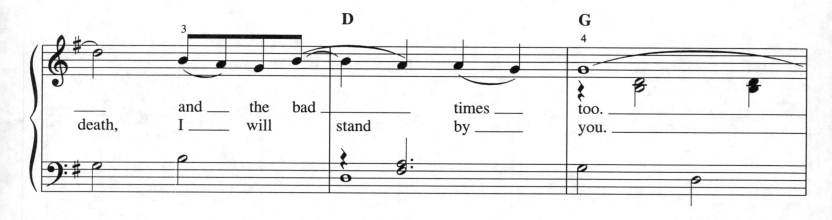

MCA music publishing

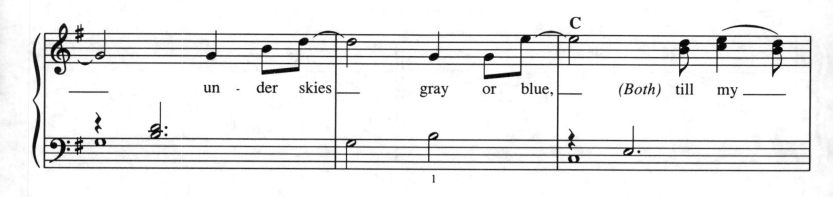

un - der skies ____ gray or blue, ____ *(Both)* till my ____

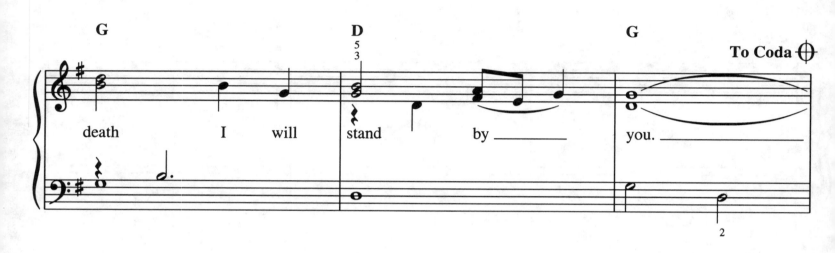

To Coda ⊕

death I will stand by _____ you. _____

____ *(Male)* There are

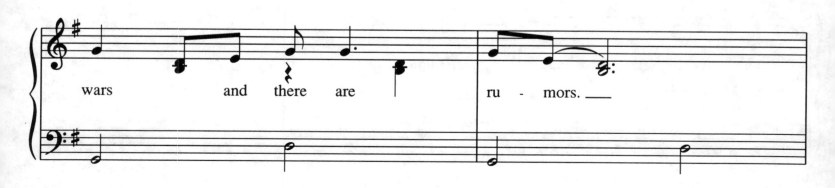

wars and there are ru - mors. ____

stand ___ by _____ you. *(Both)* I will

put on the ar - mor ___ of ___ faith - ful -

ness to fight for a heart _____ that is true. ___

___ *(Male)* Till the bat - tle is ___ won ___

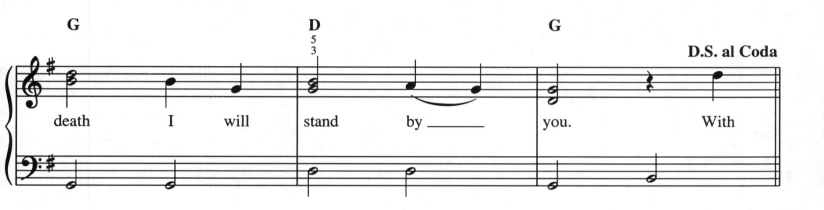

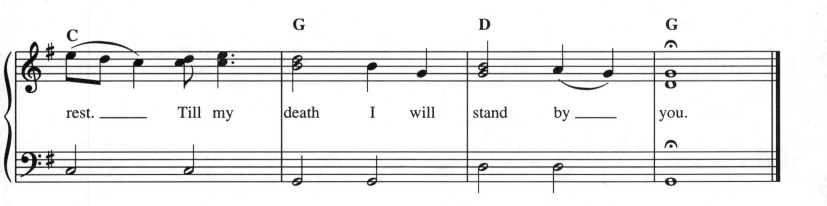

BOOT SCOOTIN' BOOGIE

Words and Music by
RONNIE DUNN

I said, get down, turn a-round, go to town, boot scoot-in'

boo-gie. Woh, get down, turn a-round,

go to town, boot scoot-in' boo-gie.

Additional Lyrics

4. The bartender asks me, says,
   "Son, what will it be?"
   I want a shot at that red head younder lookin' at me.
   The dance floor's hoppin'
   And it's hotter than the Fourth of July.
   I see outlaws, inlaws, crooks and straights
   All out makin' it shake doin' the boot scootin' boogie.

BRAND NEW MAN

Words and Music by DON COOK,
RONNIE DUNN and KIX BROOKS

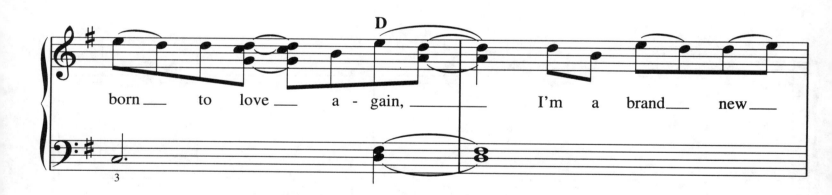

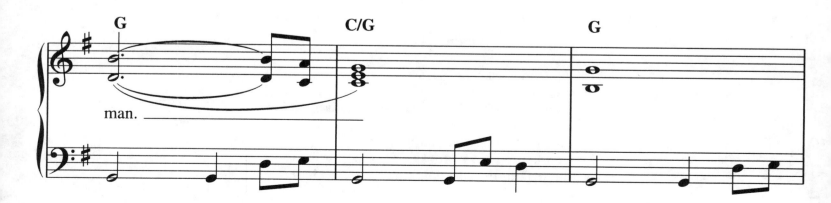

Well, the whole town's talk - in' 'bout the
love 'em and leave 'em, oh. I'd

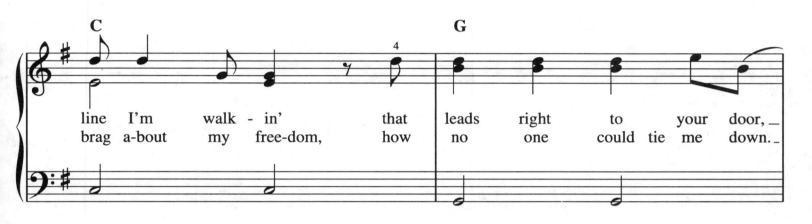

line I'm walk - in' that leads right to your door, __
brag a-bout my free-dom, how no one could tie me down. __

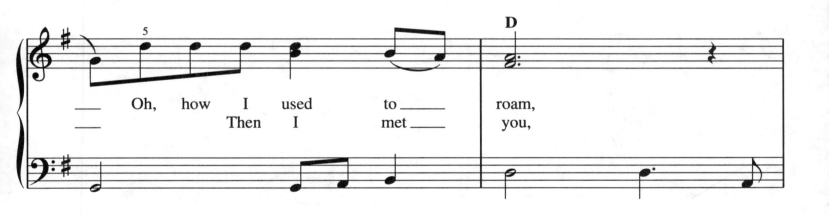

__ Oh, how I used to __ roam,
__ Then I met __ you,

I was a roll - ing stone. __
now my heart __ beats true. __ Ba - by,

I

used to have a wild ___ side, they say a coun-try mile ___ wide. I'd
you and me to-geth-er feels more ___ like for-ev-er than

D.S. Instrumental solo

burn those ___ beer ___ joints ___ down. ___ That's all ___ changed now
an-y-thing ___ I've ___ ev-er known. ___ We're right on track, ___

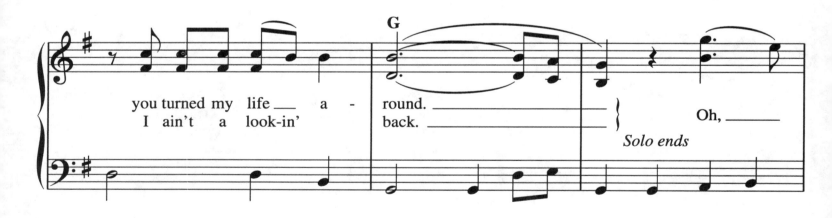

you turned my life ___ a - round. ___
I ain't a look-in' back. ___

Oh, ___

Solo ends

I saw the light, ___ I've been bap - tised by the

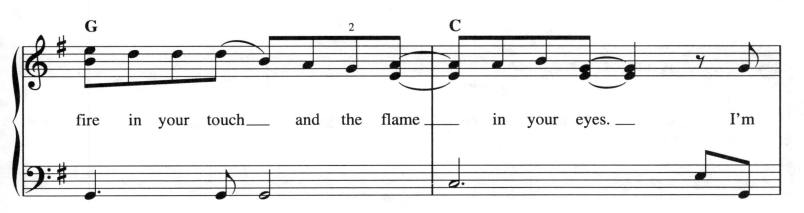

fire in your touch___ and the flame___ in your eyes. ___ I'm

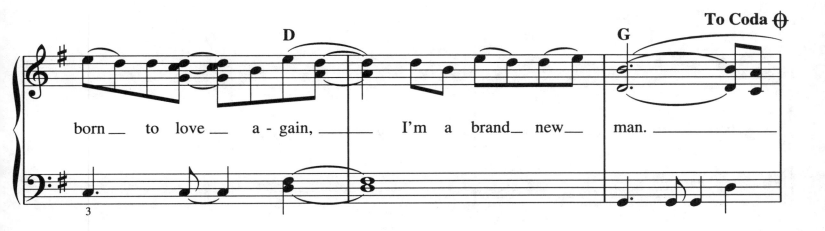

born ___ to love ___ a-gain, ___ I'm a brand___ new___ man. ___

To Coda

1.

I used to

2.

D.S. al Coda

CODA

Yeah, ___ I saw the light, ___ I've been

BLUE SUEDE SHOES

Words and Music by
CARL LEE PERKINS

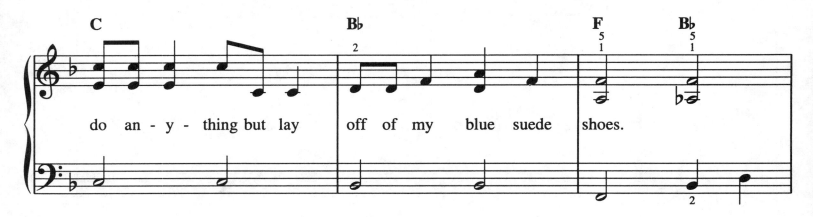

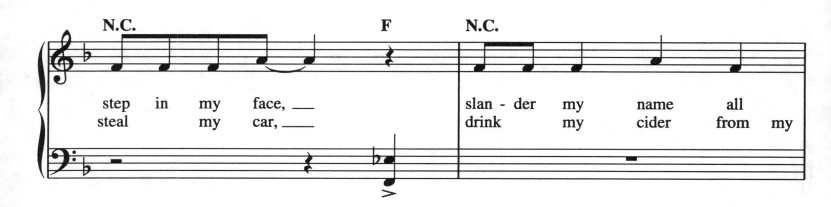

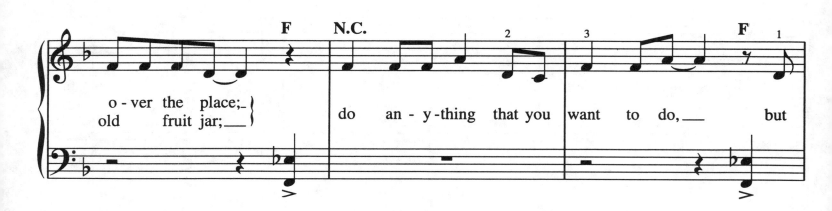

29

CHATTAHOOCHEE

Words and Music by JIM McBRIDE
and ALAN JACKSON

Bright Country 2-step

2. Well, we

1. Way down yon-der on the Chat-ta-hoo-chee it gets hot-ter than a
fogged up the win-dows in ___ my old Chev-y; I was will-in' but ___

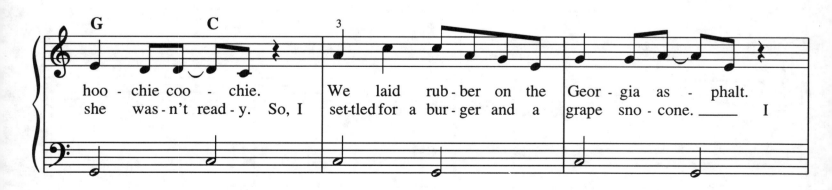

hoo-chie coo-chie. We laid rub-ber on the Geor-gia as-phalt.
she was-n't read-y. So, I set-tled for a bur-ger and a grape sno-cone. ___ I

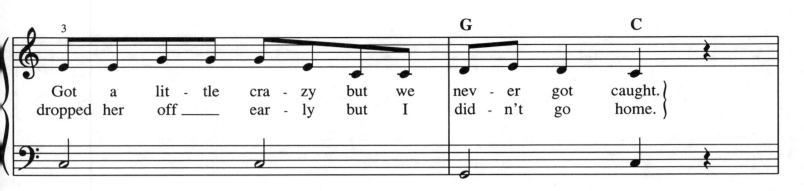

Got a lit - tle cra - zy but we nev - er got caught.
dropped her off ear - ly but I did - n't go home.

Down by the riv - er on a Fri - day night, Pyr - a - mid of cans in the

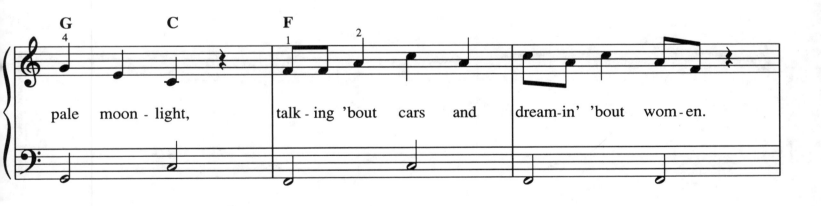

pale moon - light, talk - ing 'bout cars and dream-in' 'bout wom - en.

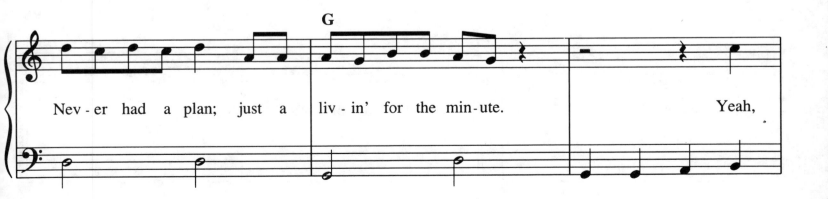

Nev - er had a plan; just a liv - in' for the min - ute. Yeah,

way down yon-der on the Chat - ta-hoo - chee; nev - er knew how much that mud-dy wa - ter

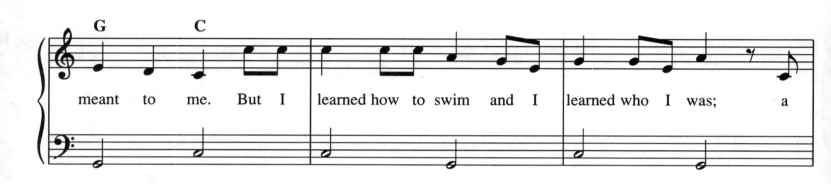

meant to me. But I learned how to swim and I learned who I was; a

1.

lot a - bout liv - in' and a lit - tle 'bout love.

2.

lit - tle 'bout love, a lot a - bout liv - in' and a lit - tle 'bout _ love.

rit.

DOWN IN THE VALLEY

Traditional American Folksong

2. Roses love sunshine, violets love dew
Angels in heaven, know I love you.
Know I love dear, know I love you.
Angels in heaven, know I love you.

3. If you don't love me, love whom you please
Throw your arms round me, give my heart ease.
Give my heart ease love, give my heart ease.
Throw your arms round me, give my heart ease.

4. Build me a castle forty feet high
So I can see him as he rides by
As he rides by love, as he rides by
So I can see him as he rides by.

5. Write me a letter, send it by mail
Send it in care of Birmingham jail.
Birmingham jail love, Birmingham jail
Send it in care of Birmingham jail.

(I Wish I Was In)
DIXIE

Words and Music by
DANIEL DECATUR EMMETT

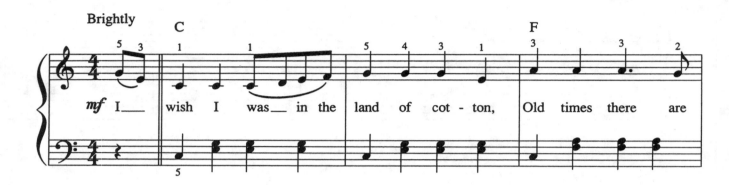

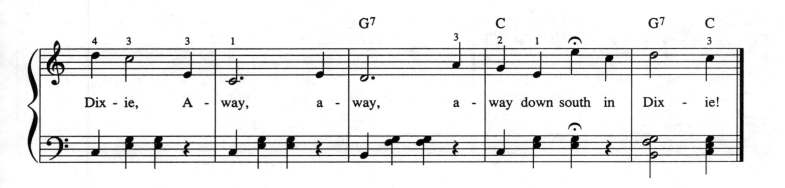

THE GAMBLER

Words and Music by
DON SCHLITZ

star - in'   out the   win - dow   at   the   dark - ness,   'til
say - in'   I can   see you're   out   of   a - ces,   for a

1.

bore - dom   o - ver - took us   and he be - gan   to   speak.   He said,

2.

taste   of   your   whis - key   I'll   give you   some   ad -

vice.   So   I   hand - ed   him   my

bot - tle and he drank down my last swal-low. Then he bummed a

cig - a - rette __ and asked me for a light. And the

night got death - ly qui - et, and his face lost all ex -

pres - sion said, "If you're gon - na play __ the game boy you got - ta

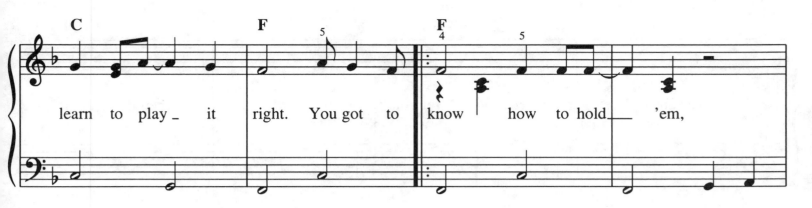

learn to play _ it right. You got to know how to hold _ 'em,

know when to fold _ 'em, know when to

walk a - way _ and know when to run. _ You nev - er

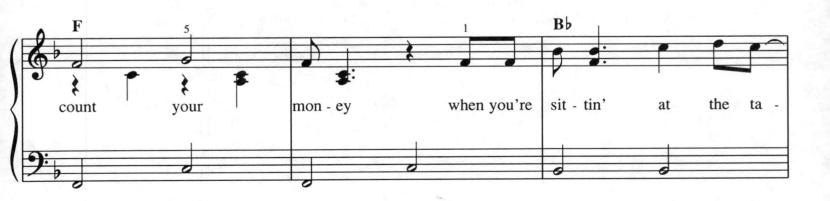

count your mon - ey when you're sit - tin' at the ta -

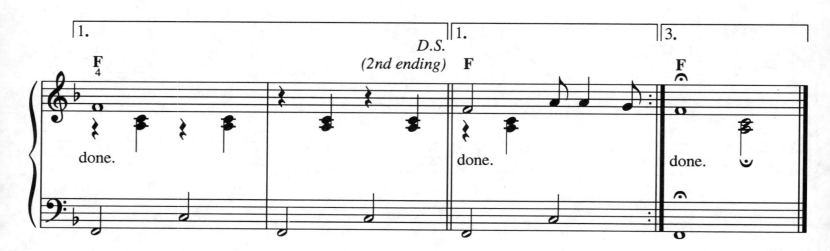

Additional Lyrics

Ev'ry gambler knows that the secret to survivin'
Is knowin' what to throw away and knowin' what to keep.
'Cause ev'ry hand's a winner and ev'ry hand's a loser
And the best that you can hope for is to die in your sleep.

And when he'd finished speakin', he turned back towards the window
Crushed out his cigarette and faded off to sleep.
And shomewhere in the darkness the gambler he broke even
But in his final words I found an ace that I could keep. You've got to...*(Chorus)*

HEARTBREAK HOTEL

Words and Music by MAE BOREN AXTON,
TOMMY DURDEN and ELVIS PRESLEY

Steady blues beat

1. Since my ba - by left me, I found a new place to dwell. Well, it's
if your ba - by leaves ya, and you've got a tale to tell, well, just

down at the end ___ of Lone - ly Street at Heart-break Ho - tel where I'll be,
take a walk ___ down Lone - ly Street to Heart-break Ho - tel where you'll be,

I'll be so lone - ly, ba - by, well, I'm so lone - ly;
you'll be so lone - ly, ba - by, you'll be so lone - ly,

I'll be so lone - ly ____ I could die. 2.,5. Al -
you'll be so lone - ly ____ you could die.

though it's al - ways crowd - ed you still can find some room for
bell - hop's tears are flow - in', the desk clerk's dressed in black. They

bro - ken heart - ed lov - ers to cry a - way their gloom. __
been so long __ on Lone - ly Street they ain't nev - er gon - na come back. __ They get so

GOLDEN RING

Words and Music by BOBBY BRADDOCK
and RAFE VAN HOY

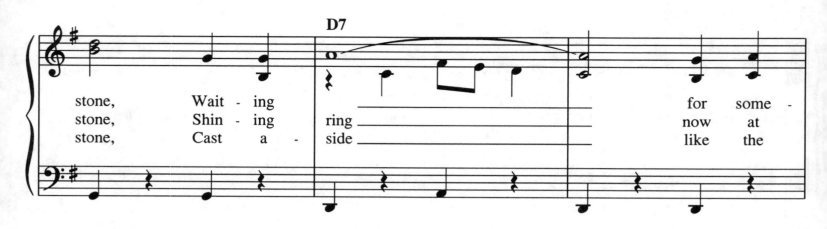

stone, Wait - ing
stone, Shin - ing ring _____ now at
stone, Cast a - side _____ like the
for some -

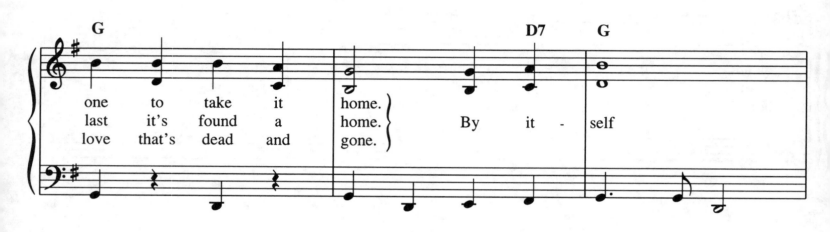

one to take it home.
last it's found a home.
love that's dead and gone.
By it - self

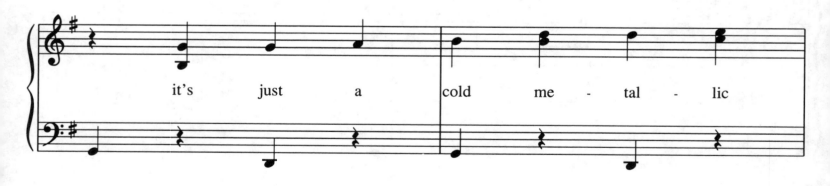

it's just a cold me - tal - lic

thing, On - ly love can make a gold - en wed-ding

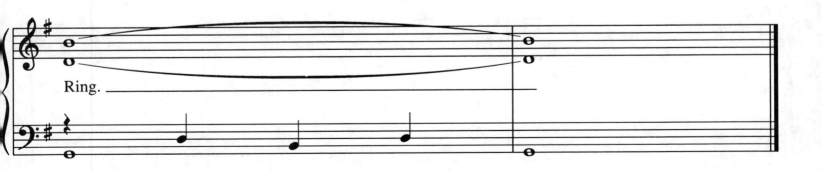

A GOOD HEARTED WOMAN

Words and Music by WAYLON JENNINGS
and WILLIE NELSON

good life he prom - ised
par - ty's all o - ver
ain't what she's
she'll wel - come

liv - ing____ to - day.____
him back home a - gain.____

But she nev - er com -
Lord knows she don't un - der -

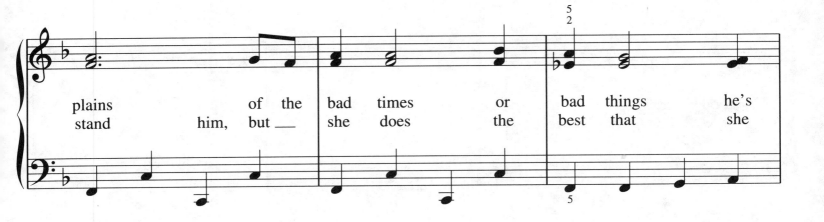

plains of the bad times or
stand him, but ____ she does the
bad things he's
best that she

done, Lord.
can.

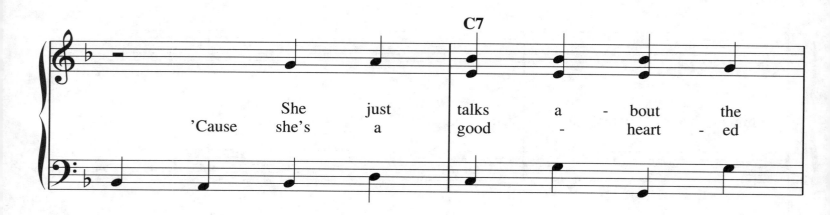

'Cause She just talks a - bout the
'Cause she's a good - heart - ed

good times they've had and all the
wom - an she loves her

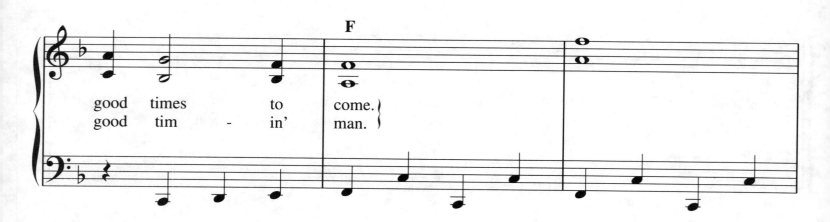

good times to come.
good tim - in' man.

spite   of   his   ways   that   she   don't   un - der -

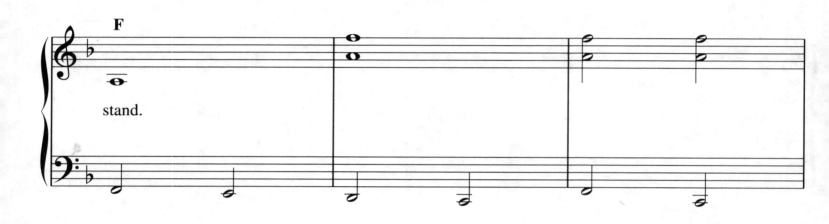

stand.

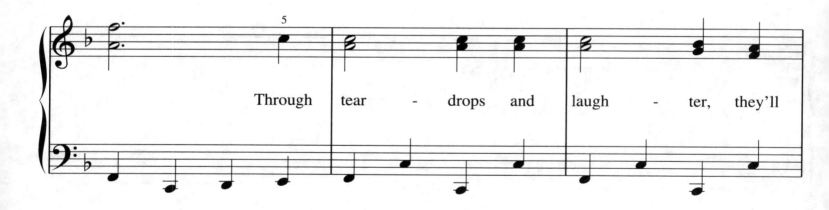

Through   tear - drops   and   laugh - ter,   they'll

pass   through   this   world   hand   in   hand,

a

C7

good - heart - ed wom - an

lov - in' her

F

good - tim - in' man.

1.

2.

D.S. and Fade

She's a

HONEY

Words and Music by
BOBBY RUSSELL

Moderately

See the tree how big it's grown, but friend it has-n't been too long it
She was al-ways young at heart, ___ kind-a dumb and kind-a smart and I

with pedal

was-n't big. I laughed at her and she got mad, the
loved her so. I sur-prised her with a pup-py,

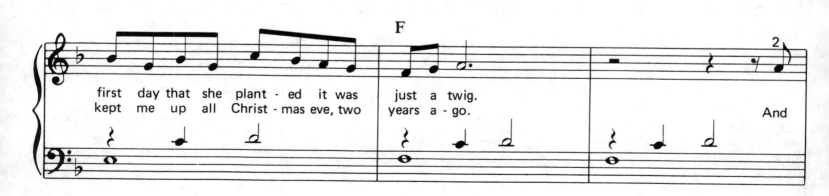

first day that she plant-ed it was just a twig.
kept me up all Christ-mas eve, two years a-go. And

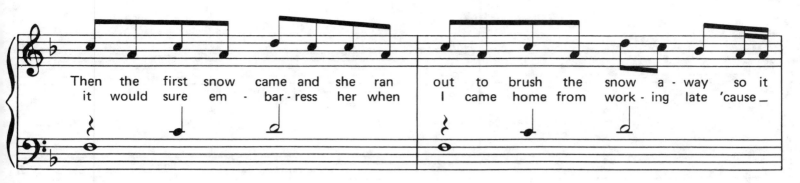

Then the first snow came and she ran out to brush the snow a-way so it
it would sure em-bar-ress her when I came home from work-ing late 'cause_

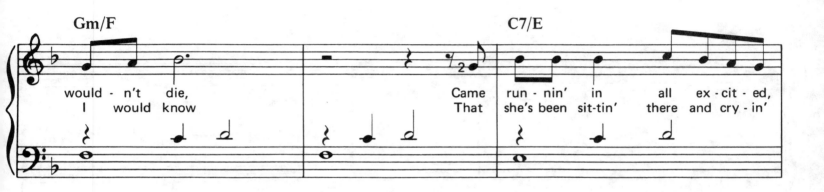

Gm/F   C7/E

would-n't die,   Came run-nin' in all ex-cit-ed,
I would know   That she's been sit-tin' there and cry-in'

1. F

slipped and al-most hurt her-self, I laughed 'til I cried._
o-ver some_ sad and sil-ly

2. F   *Chorus*
                                                  Gm

late, late show.   And Hon-ey, I miss you.

and I'm be-ing good ____ And I love to be

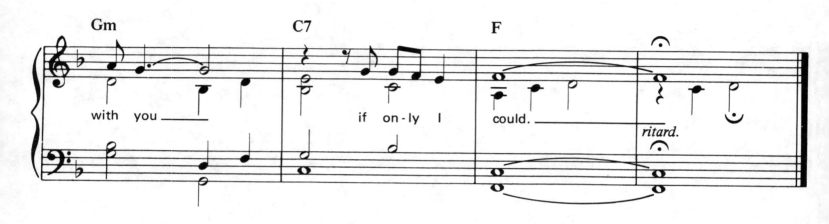

with you ____ if on-ly I could. ____ *ritard.*

3rd Verse: She wrecked the car and she was sad
And so afraid that I'd be mad,
But what the heck.
Though I pretended hard to be,
Guess she could say she saw through me
And hugged my neck.

I came home unexpectedly
And found her crying needlessly
In the middle of the day,
And it was in the early spring,
When flowers bloom and robins sing
She went away.
To Chorus

4th Verse: Yes, one day, while I wasn't home,
While she was there and all alone
The angels came.
Now all I have is memories of Honey,
And I wake up nights and call her name.

Now my life's an empty stage,
Where Honey lived and Honey played,
And love grew up.
A small cloud passes over head
And cries down in the flower bed
That Honey loved.
To Chorus

HERE'S A QUARTER
(Call Someone Who Cares)

Words and Music by
TRAVIS TRITT

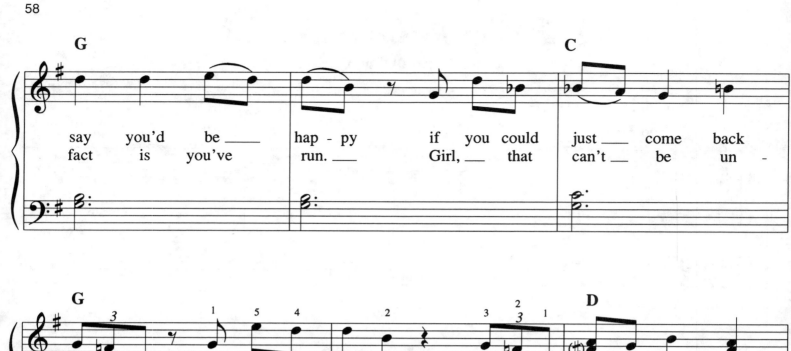

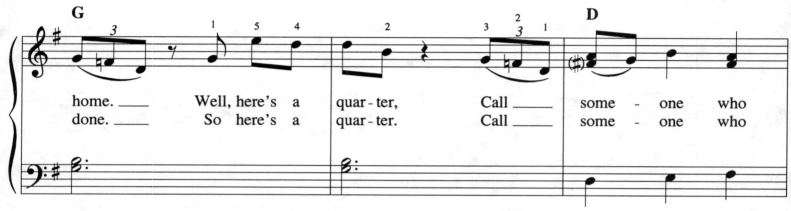

D.S. al Coda

CODA

I FEEL LUCKY

Words and Music by MARY CHAPIN CARPENTER
and DON SCHLITZ

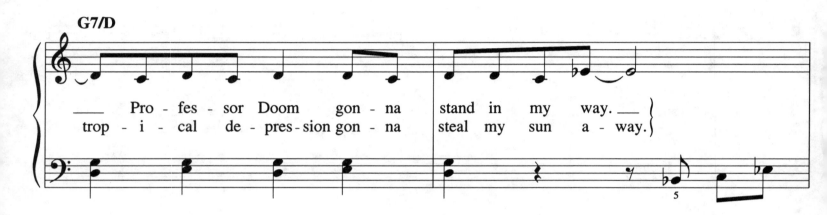

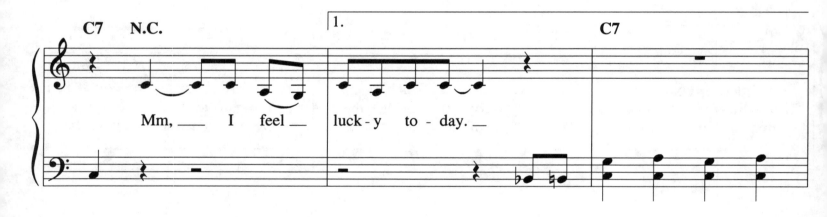

JAMBALAYA
(On the Bayou)

Words and Music by
HANK WILLIAMS

Bright Cajun beat

Good- bye

Joe, me got- ta go, me oh, my oh,
daux, Fon- tain- eaux, the place is buzz- in',
down far from town get me a pi- rogue,

Me got- ta go, pole the pi- rogue down the
Kin- folk come to see Y- vonne by the
And I'll catch all the fish in the

bay- ou.
doz- en.
bay- ou.

My Y- vonne, the sweet- est
Dress in style and go hog
Swap my mon to buy Y-

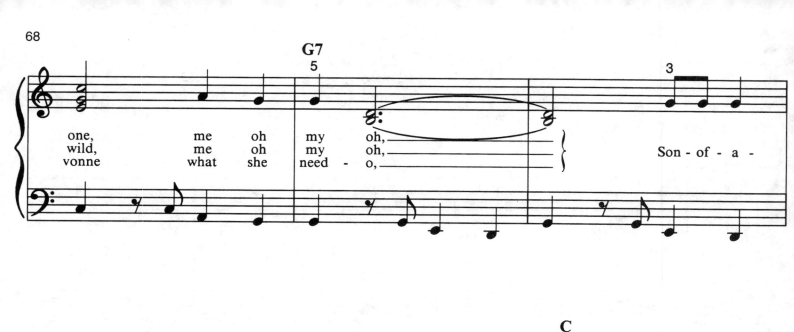

G7

one,   me oh   my   oh,_____ Son - of - a -
wild,   me oh   my   oh,_____
vonne   what   she   need - o,_____

C

gun,   we'll have   big   fun   on   the   bay - ou._____

____ Jam - ba - la - ya   and   a   craw - fish   pie   and   fil - let

G7

gum - bo,_____ 'cause to - night I'm gon - na

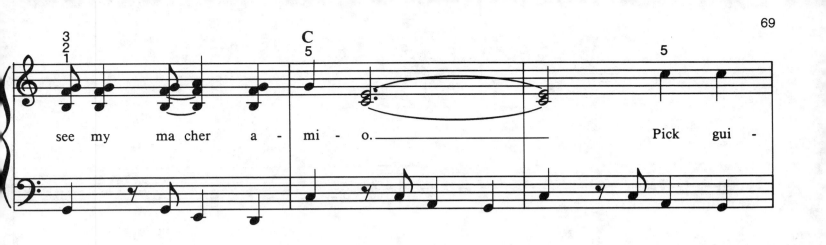

see my ma cher a - mi - o._____ Pick gui -

tar, fill fruit jar, and be gay - o;_____

_____ Son - of - a gun we'll have big fun on the

bay - ou._____ Thi - bo - bay - ou._____
Set - tle

IT'S HARD TO BE HUMBLE

Words and Music by
MAC DAVIS

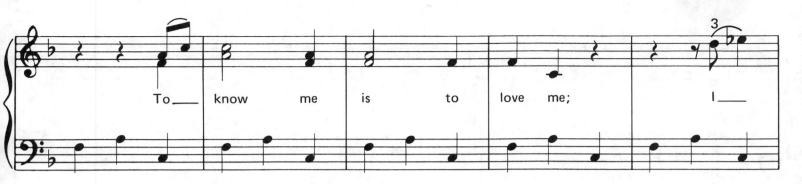

To___ know me is to love me; I___

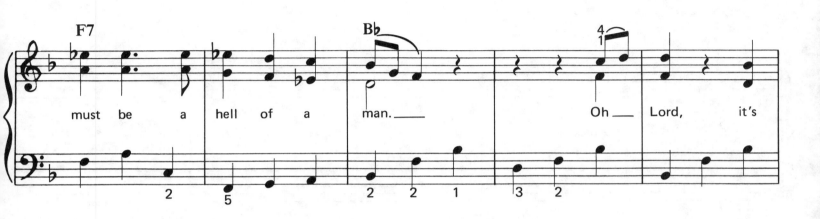

must be a hell of a man.___ Oh___ Lord, it's

hard to be hum - ble,_____ But I'm do - in' the

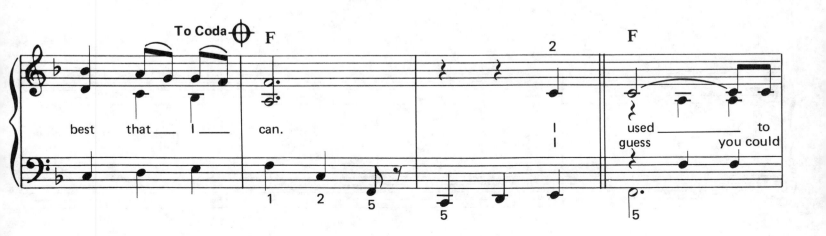

best that___ I___ can.

used_____ to
guess_____ you could

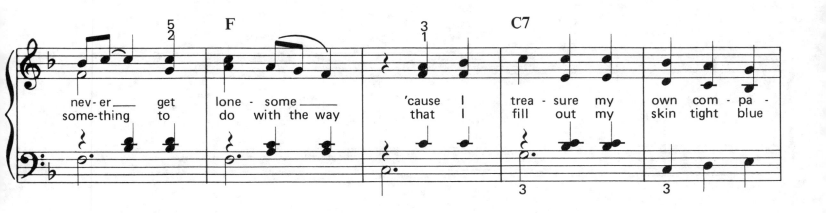

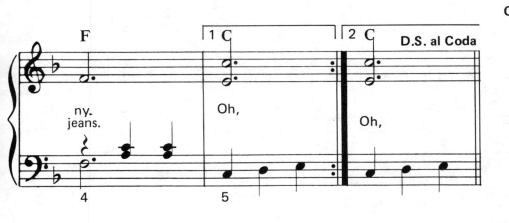

KING OF THE ROAD

Words and Music by
ROGER MILLER

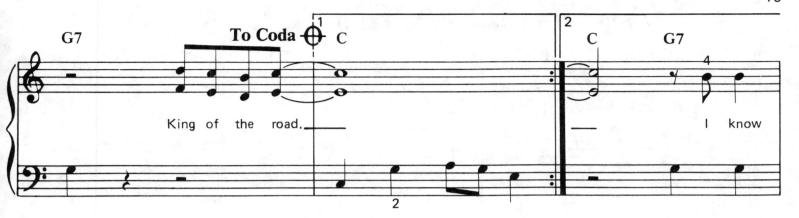

King of the road.___ I know

ev-er-y en-gi-neer on ev-er-y train,___ all of the chil - dren and

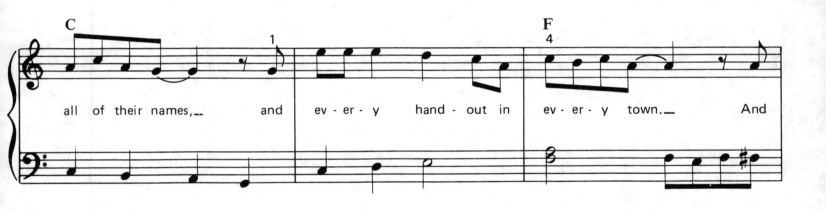

all of their names,___ and ev-er-y hand-out in ev-er-y town.___ And

ev'-ry lock that ain't locked when no one's a-round.___ I sing

MAKE THE WORLD GO AWAY

Words and Music by
HANK COCHRAN

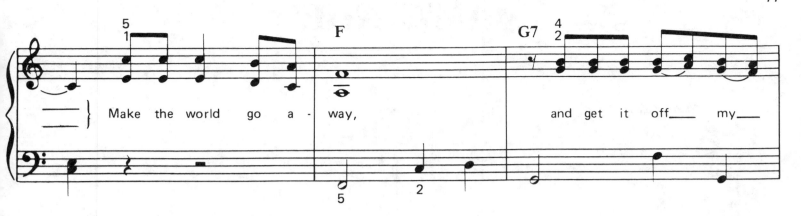

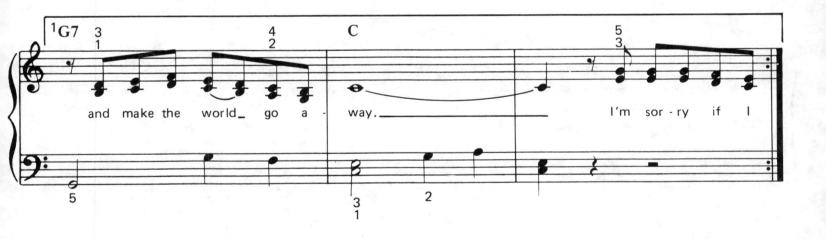

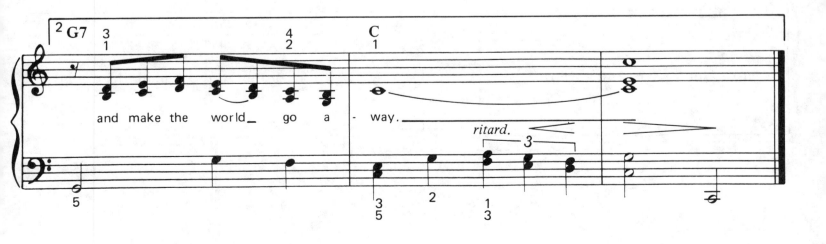

MAMA TRIED

Words and Music by
MERLE HAGGARD

The first thing I re-mem-ber know-in' was a

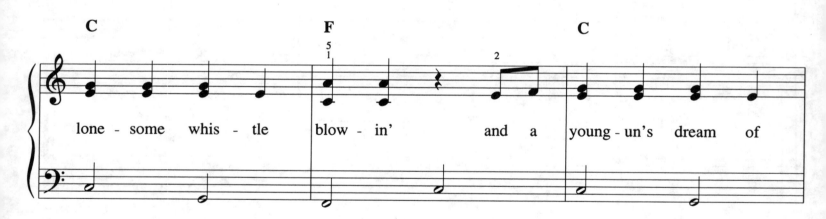

lone-some whis-tle blow-in' and a young-un's dream of

grow-in' up to ride, on a freight train leav-in'

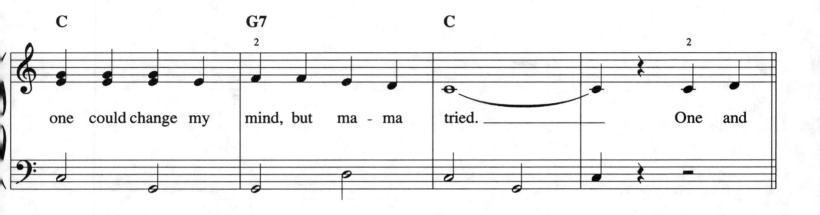

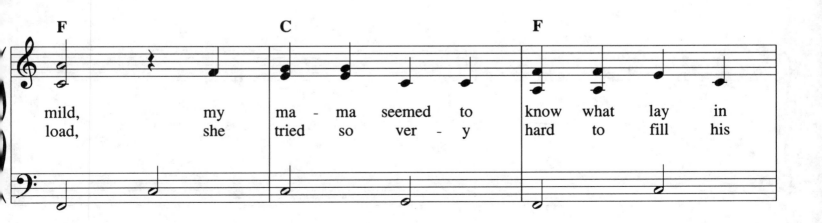

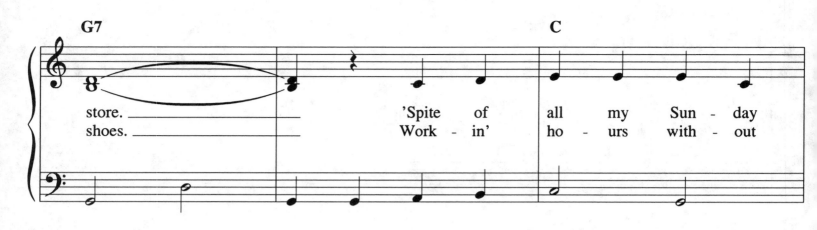

store. _____ 'Spite of all my Sun - day
shoes. _____ Work - in' ho - urs with - out

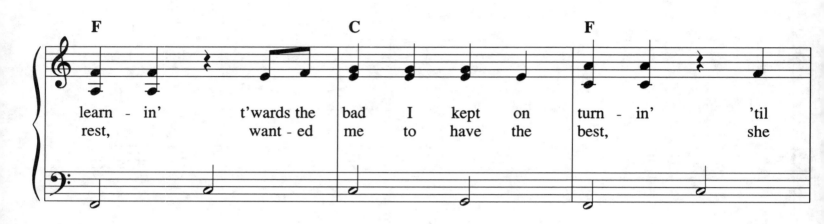

learn - in' t'wards the bad I kept on turn - in' 'til
rest, want - ed me to have the best, she

ma - ma could - n't hold me an - y - more. _____
tried to raise me right but I re - fused. _____

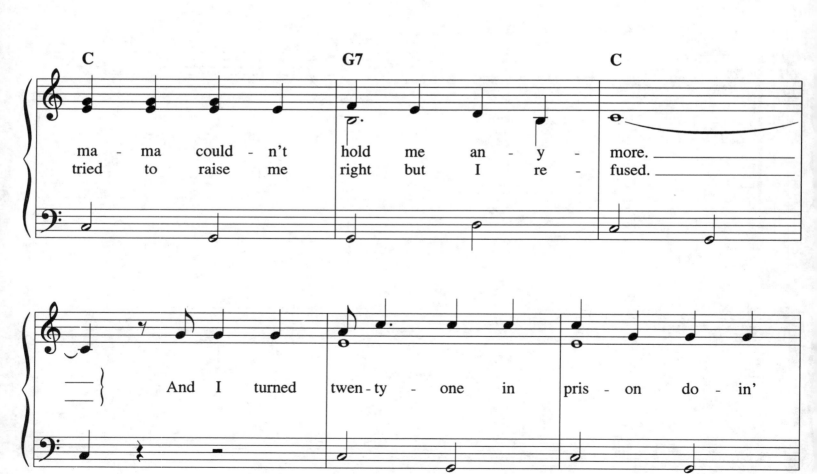

And I turned twen - ty - one in pris - on do - in'

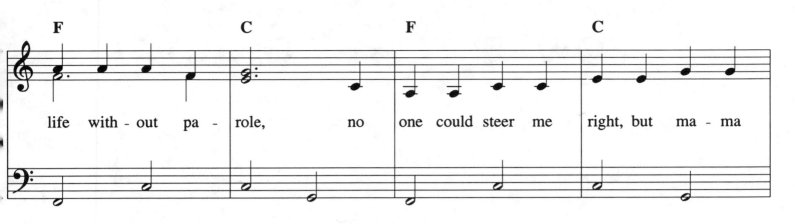

life with - out pa - role,   no one could steer me right, but ma - ma

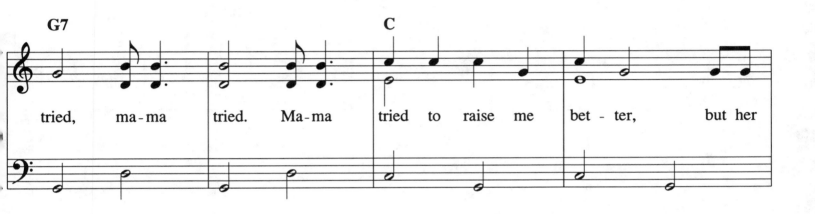

tried, ma - ma tried. Ma - ma tried to raise me bet - ter, but her

plead - ing I de - nied. That leaves on - ly me to blame, 'cause ma - ma

tried. _____   Dear ol' | tried. _____

MAMMAS DON'T LET YOUR BABIES GROW UP TO BE COWBOYS

Words and Music by ED BRUCE
and PATSY BRUCE

Country Waltz

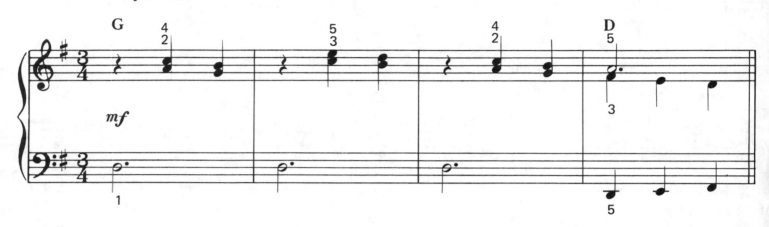

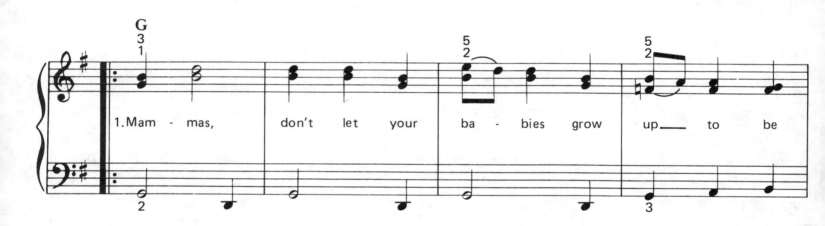

1. Mam - mas, don't let your ba - bies grow up___ to be

cow - boys.

Don't
'Cause they'll

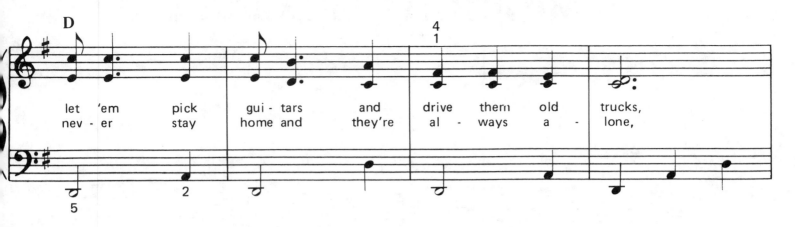

Verse 2.

A cowboy ain't easy to love and he's harder to hold
And it means more to him to give you a song than silver and gold.

Budweiser buckles and soft faded Levis
And each night begins a new day.
If you can't understand him and he don't die young
He'll probably just ride away.

Verse 3.

A cowboy loves smoky ole pool rooms and clear mountain mornings
Little warm puppies and children and girls of the night.

Then that don't know him won't like him
And them that do sometimes won't know how to take him.
He's not wrong, he's just diff'rent
And his pride won't let him do things to make you think he's right.

MIDNIGHT SPECIAL

Traditional

And if you say a thing a - bout it,_____ you're in trou - ble with the
And you can bet your bot - tom dol - lar._____ you're for Su - gar - land___

Chorus

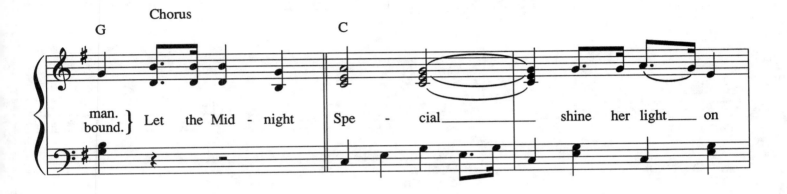

man.
bound. } Let the Mid - night Spe - cial_____ shine her light___ on

me, Let the Mid - night Spe - cial_____

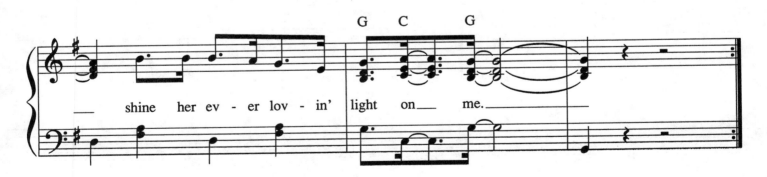

shine her ev - er lov - in' light on___ me._____

3. Lord, Thelma said she loved me, but I believe she told a lie,
   'Cause she hasn't been to see me since last July.
   She brought me little coffee, she brought me little tea,
   She brought me nearly everything but the jail house key.

MY ELUSIVE DREAMS

Words and Music by CURLY PUTMAN
and BILLY SHERRILL

SWINGIN'

Words and Music by JOHN DAVID ANDERSON
and LIONEL A. DELMORE

With a strong beat

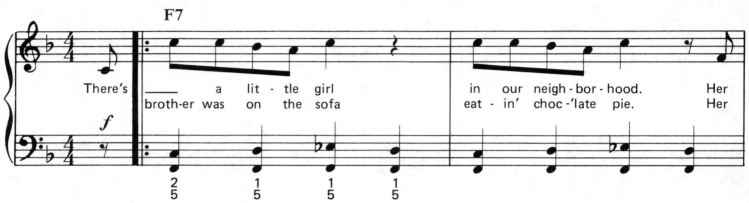

o - ver to her house _____ and this was go - in' on: Her
on the porch with Char - lotte feel-in'

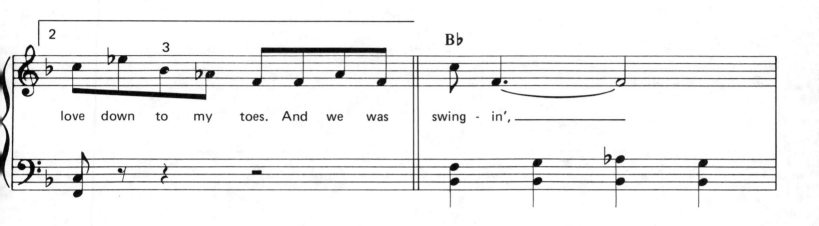

love down to my toes. And we was swing - in', _____

swing - in', yes, we was swing - in' _____

swing - in'. _____ Lit - tle Char - lotte, she's as pret - ty as the

an - gels when they sing; I can't be - lieve I'm out here on her

front porch in the swing, just a swing - in', _____

swing - in', _____ swing - in', _____

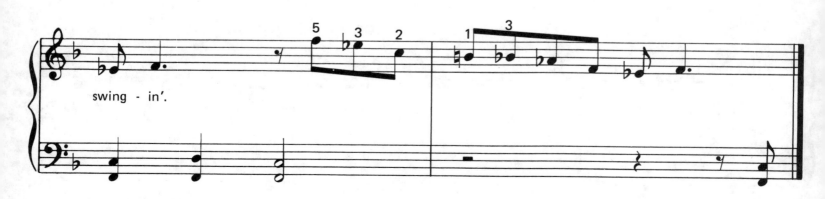

swing - in'.

SHENANDOAH

American Folksong

2. O Shenandoah, I love your daughter,
   Away, you rolling river,
   For her I've crossed the rolling water,
   Away, I'm bound away,
   Across the wide Missouri.

3. The trader loved this Indian maiden,
   Away, you rolling river,
   With presents his canoe was laden,
   Away I'm bound away,
   Across the wide Missouri.

4. O Shenandoah, I'm bound to leave you,
   Away, you rolling river,
   O Shenandoah, I'll not deceive you.
   Away, I'm bound away,
   Across the wide Missouri.

5. O Shenandoah, I long to hear you,
   Away, you rolling river,
   O Shenandoah, I long to hear you.
   Away, I'm bound away,
   Across the wide Missouri.

SONG OF THE SOUTH

Words and Music by
BOB McDILL

(Sing it)   Song,

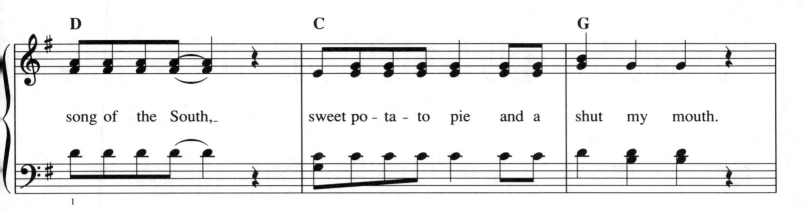

song of the South,   sweet po - ta - to pie and a shut my mouth.

Gone, gone with the wind,   There ain't no - bod-y look-in'

To Coda ⊕

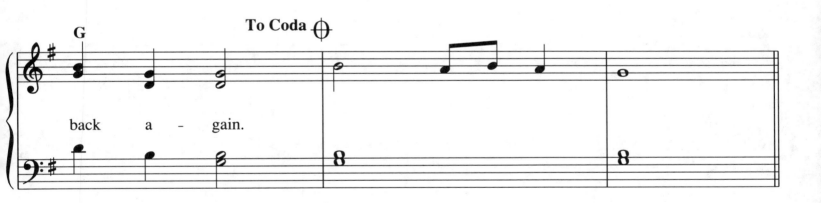

back a - gain.

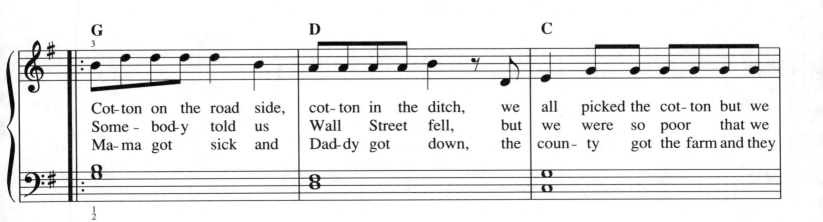

Cot-ton on the road side, cot-ton in the ditch, we all picked the cot-ton but we
Some - bod-y told us Wall Street fell, but we were so poor that we
Ma-ma got sick and Dad-dy got down, the coun-ty got the farm and they

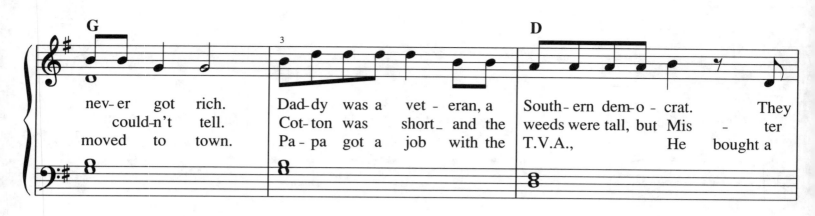

nev-er got rich.
Dad-dy was a vet-eran, a
South-ern dem-o-crat. They

could-n't tell.
Cot-ton was short and the
weeds were tall, but Mis - ter

moved to town.
Pa-pa got a job with the
T.V.A., He bought a

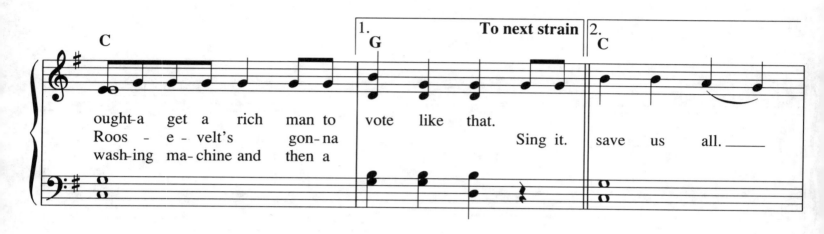

1.
To next strain
2.

ought-a get a rich man to
vote like that.
Sing it.
save us all. _____

Roos - e - velt's gon-na
Sing it.

wash-ing ma-chine and then a

3.

Well Chev - ro - let.

Sing it.
Song,

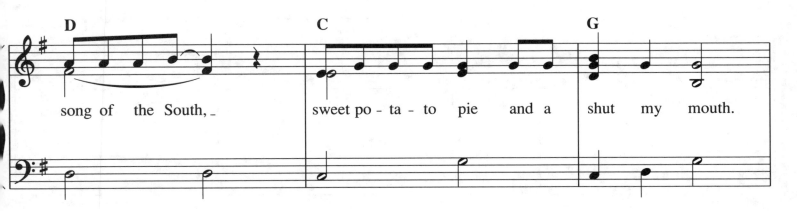

song of the South, — sweet po - ta - to pie and a shut my mouth.

Gone, gone with the wind, — there ain't no - bod - y look - in'

back a - gain.

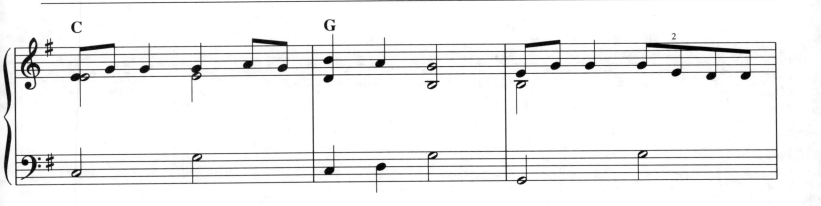

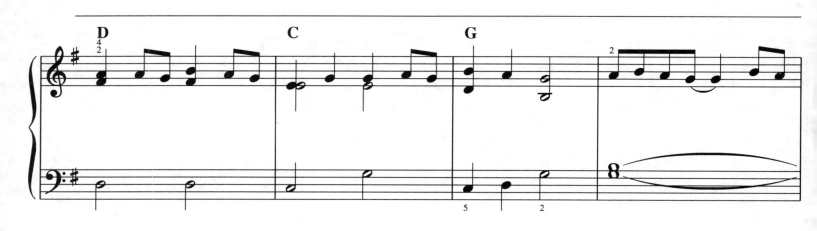

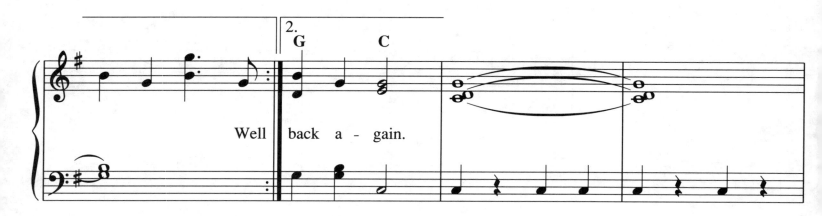

Well back a - gain.

D.S. al Coda

Play it

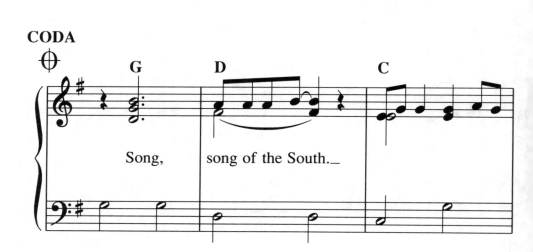

CODA

Song, song of the South.

Gone, gone with the wind,

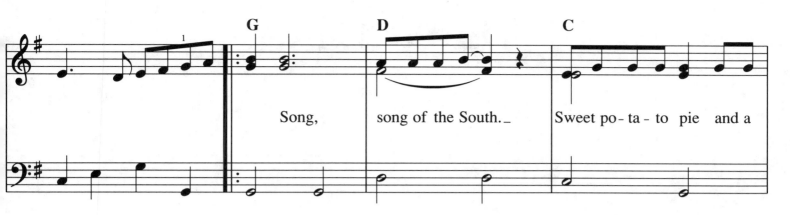

Song, song of the South._ Sweet po - ta - to pie and a

shut my mouth. Song, song of the South, _

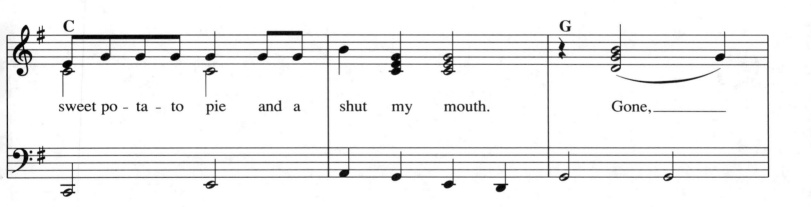

sweet po - ta - to pie and a shut my mouth. Gone,_____

gone with the wind, _ Ain't no - bod-y look-in' back a - gain.

(Let Me Be Your)
TEDDY BEAR

Words and Music by KAL MANN
and BERNIE LOWE

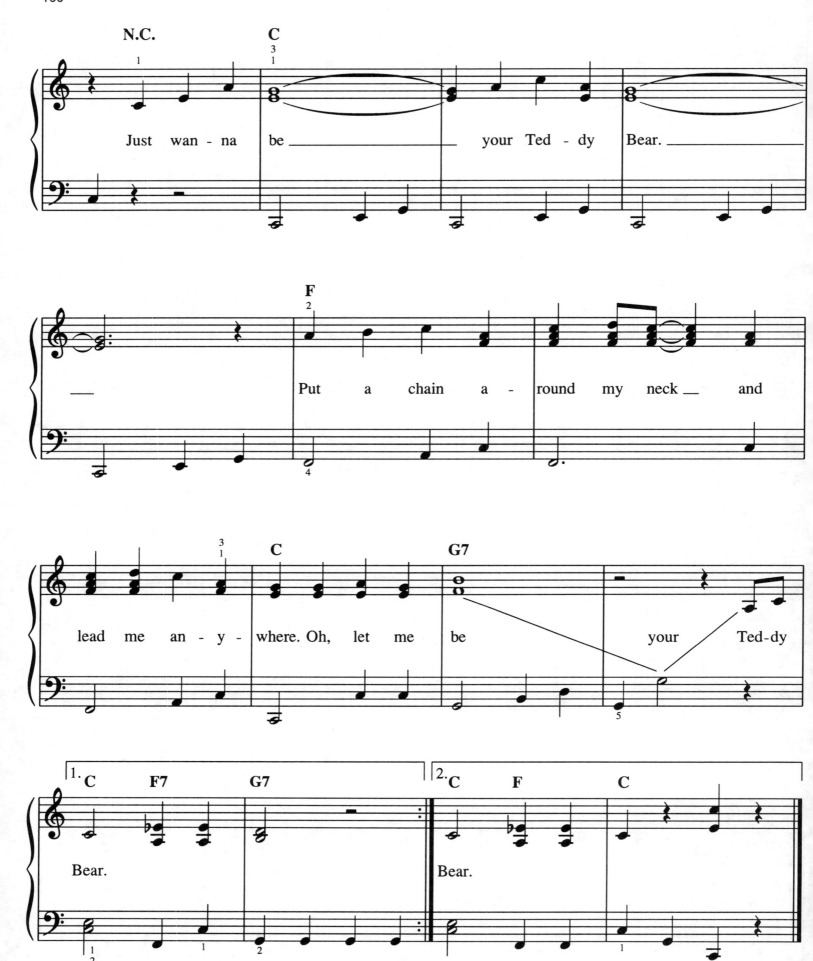

T-R-O-U-B-L-E

Words and Music by
JERRY CHESNUT

Fast Country/Rock

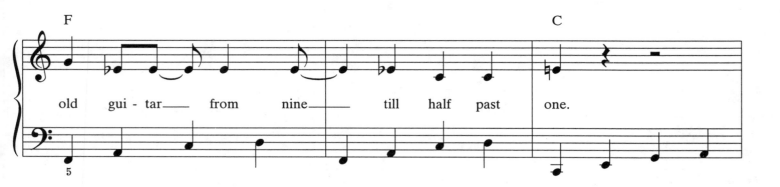

TOO MUCH

Words and Music by LEE ROSENBERG
and BERNIE WEINMAN

1. Hon - ey, I ___ love you too much,
2. You spend all my mon - ey too much.
3.-4. *See additional lyrics*

need ___ your ___ lov - in' too much.
Have to share you, hon - ey, too much.

Want ___ the ___ thrill of your touch.
When I want some lov - in', you're gone.

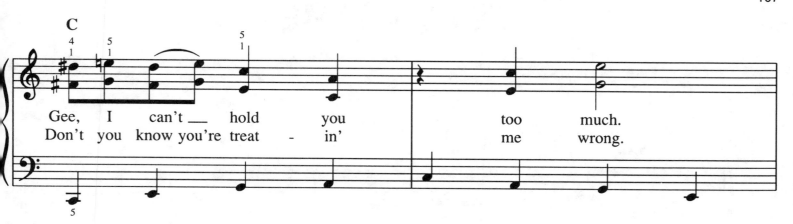

C

Gee, I can't __ hold you too much.
Don't you know you're treat - in' me wrong.

G7   F7

You do all the liv - in' while __ I do all the giv - in' 'cause I
Now you got me start - ed, don't you leave me brok - en - heart - ed 'cause I

C   1.-3.   4.

love you too much.
love you too much.   much.   *sfz*

Additional Lyrics

3. Need your lovin' all the time.
   Need your huggin', please be mine.
   Need you near me, stay real close.
   Please, please hear me, you're the most.
   Now you got me started, don't you leave me broken-hearted
   'Cause I love you too much.

4. Ev'ry time I kiss your sweet lips,
   I can feel my heart go flip, flip.
   I'm such a fool for your charms.
   Take me back, my baby, in your arms.
   Like to hear you sighin' even though I know you're lyin'
   'Cause I love you too much.

TULSA TIME

Words and Music by
DANNY FLOWERS

With a steady beat

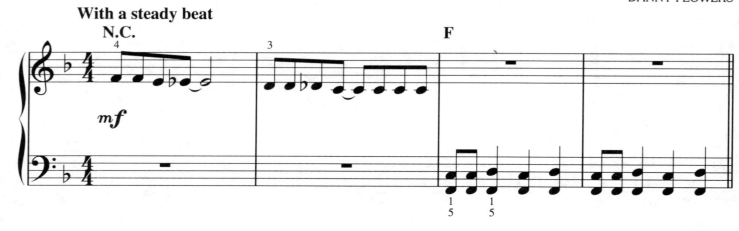

I left Ok - la - ho - ma   driv - in' in a Pon - ti - ac
there I was in Hol - ly - wood   wish - in' I was do - in' good,

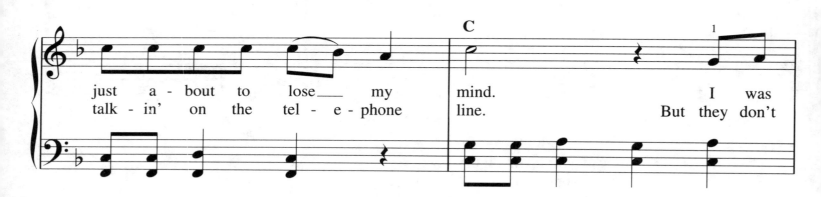

just a - bout to lose___ my   mind.   I was
talk - in' on the tel - e - phone   line.   But they don't

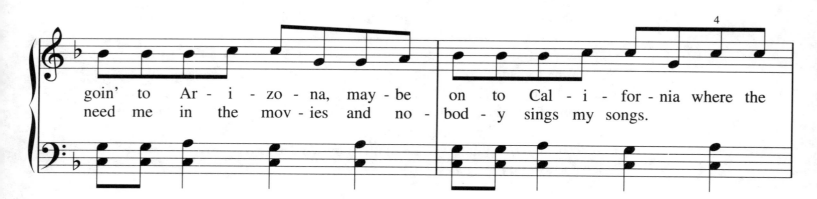

goin' to Ar - i - zo - na, may - be   on to Cal - i - for - nia where the
need me in the mov - ies and no -   bod - y sings my songs.

peo - ple all live ___ so fine. My
Guess I'm just wast - in' time. Well,

ba - by said I's cra - zy, my Mom-ma called me la - zy. I was
then I got to think-in', man, I'm real - ly sink-in' and I

goin' to show 'em all ___ this time. 'Cause you
real - ly had a flash ___ this time. I

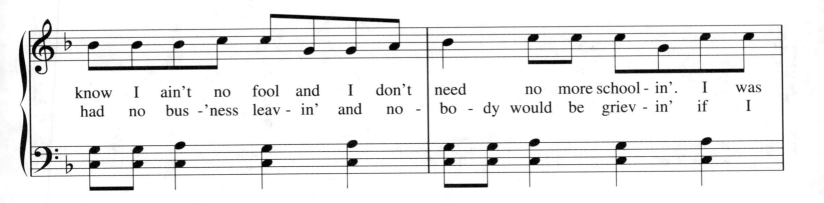

know I ain't no fool and I don't need no more school - in'. I was
had no bus - 'ness leav - in' and no - bo - dy would be griev - in' if I

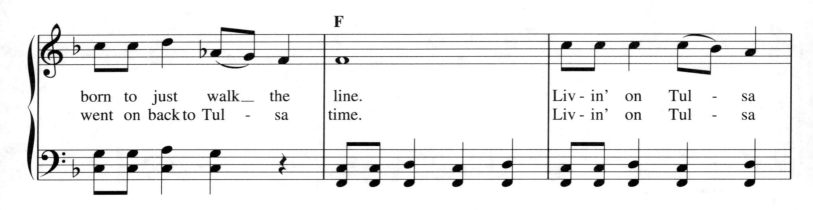

born to just walk __ the line.
went on back to Tul - sa time.
Liv - in' on Tul - sa
Liv - in' on Tul - sa

time.
time.
Liv - in' on Tul - sa time.
Liv - in' on Tul - sa time.
Well, you
Gon -na

know   I been through it when I
set my watch back to it, 'cause you
set my watch back to it.
know   I've been through it.

Liv - in' on Tul - sa   time.   Well,
Liv - in' on Tul - sa
1.
2.
time.

THE WABASH CANNON BALL

Hobo Song

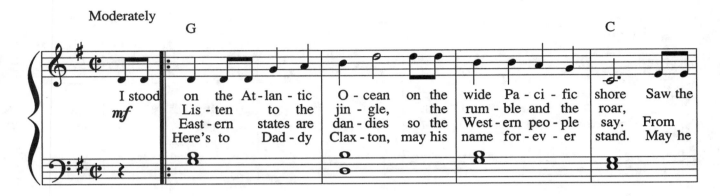

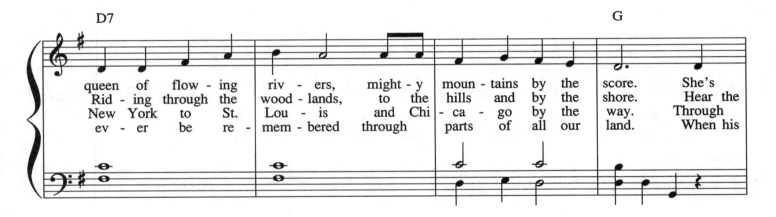

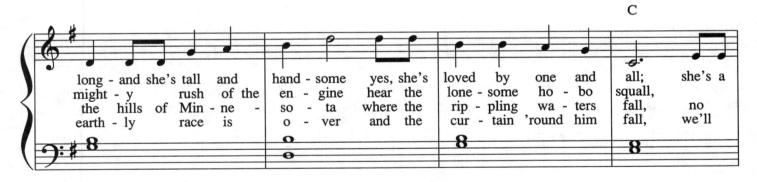

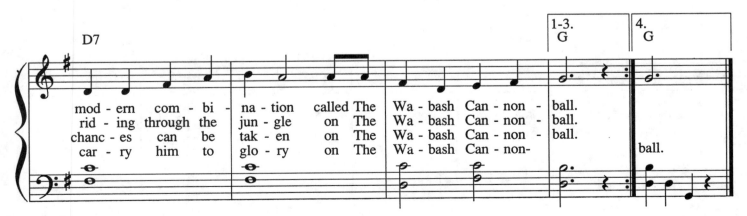

THE YELLOW ROSE OF TEXAS

Traditional Folksong